SEAWAY TRAIL LIGHTHOUSES

An Illustrated Guide
3rd Edition

to the
Historic Lighthouses Along New York State's
Great Lakes, Niagara and St. Lawrence Rivers
and Pennsylvania's Lake Erie Shoreline

Authors:
James Tinney
Mary Burdette-Watkins

Illustrators:
Leo Kuschel
David L. Tousey

Editor/Designer:
Kara Lynn Dunn

Publisher:
Seaway Trail Foundation, Inc.
P.O. Box 660, Sackets Harbor, NY 13685
1-800-SEAWAY-T

ACKNOWLEDGMENTS

This guide is based in part upon the series of lighthouse articles found in the 1989 *JOURNEY Magazine & Directory to NYS' Seaway Trail* published by Seaway Trail, Inc.. For those articles, we are indebted to F. Ross Holland, Jr., author of *America's Lighthouses* (Dover, 1988) and *Great American Lighthouses* (Preservation Press, 1989), who supplied historic background and edited the first edition. Sincere thanks also go to the dedicated individuals at the lights, the many town and county historians, United States Coast Guard personnel, and others who provided the data necessary to complete the text for all three editions. Seaway Trail, Inc. is fortunate to have found the skills and patience within Jim Tinney and Mary Burdette who generously gave their time and expertise to be principal authors of this guidebook. This third edition was updated by Kara Lynn Dunn in cooperation with the lightkeepers and owners of the Seaway Trail's historic beacons.

Published by:
SEAWAY TRAIL FOUNDATION, INC.
P.O. Box 660
Sackets Harbor, NY 13685
1-800-SEAWAY-T, 315-646-1000

Byron C. Gale, Chairman, Seaway Trail Foundation, Inc.
Charles Krupke, President, Seaway Trail, Inc.
Teresa H. Mitchell, Executive Director, Seaway Trail, Inc.
and Seaway Trail Foundation, Inc.

New York State Legislative Advisors:
Senator John A. DeFrancisco, Assemblyman Paul A. Tokasz

*This successful series of Seaway Trail Lighthouse guidebook editions
has been partially funded by the New York State Legislature
through the NYS Office of Parks, Recreation and Historic Preservation
and by a federal Intermodal Surface Transportation Efficiency Act grant
through the NYS Department of Transportation.*

Table of Contents

INTRODUCTION

Welcome to the scenic Seaway Trail and its historic lighthouses. The Trail, 504 miles in length, follows four major waterways in upstate New York and Pennsylvania— Lake Erie, the Niagara River, Lake Ontario and the St. Lawrence River. The Seaway Trail, already America's longest designated National Recreation Trail, became a National Scenic Byway in September 1996. The Seaway Trail is suitable for driving, motorcoach touring, bicycling, and pleasure boating. Conveniently accessible to the New York State Canal Recreationway system, boaters can reach and explore the Seaway Trail from any of the Great Lakes as well as from New York City and Montreal.

Along the shores of the Seaway Trail, from the Barcelona Light on Lake Erie to the Ogdensburg Harbor Light on the St. Lawrence River, you'll see more than two dozen lighthouses, each uniquely pleasing to the eye, and steeped in fascinating history. Whether built of stone or wood, in the Gothic Revival or Shingle Style, placed on a bluff overlooking a busy harbor or on a rocky, isolated, river island, each light has its own unforgettable mystique. The first edition of this guidebook was offered in the bicentennial year of America's Federal Lighthouse Act to help you enjoy and appreciate the architectural, historic and scenic individuality of each light along our route. The continuing popularity of lighthouses and this Seaway Trail Lighthouses guidebook led to a second, and, now an expanded third edition of the book.

The entire length of the Seaway Trail has a rich and varied cultural heritage. During the colonial period, the French and English alike vied for control of this strategically important region. Each culture made its mark on the land and its people—a legacy which remains today and is reflected in our architecture, historic sites, cultural events, and traditional ethnic cuisine.

In the wake of the American Revolution, Great Lakes Erie and Ontario became prime transportation routes for the nation. The building of lighthouses along what is today known as the Seaway Trail went hand-in-hand with our nation's economic growth. The waters and the lighthouses formed a perfect marriage that would last for close to a century. As enormous shipments of grain, lumber and coal traveled eastward on the rivers and lakes, finished goods, transported by sailing vessel and later by steamship, passed them heading west. By the early nineteenth century, the Great Lakes had become the most important single transportation system in the United States.

With the opening of the Erie Canal in 1825, a direct, cheap route between the Midwest and the Atlantic Coast was made available. The year 1855 saw the completion of the shipping canal at Sault Ste. Marie and the linking of Lake Superior with the lower Great Lakes. Soon large quantities of iron ore and copper were on their way to factories in the east.

By the time of the Civil War, the Great Lakes system moved the nation's economy, shipping natural resources and agricultural products from America's heartland and manufactured goods from the industrialized Northeast.

Lighthouses were constructed to either mark the entry to a river or harbor, or to warn mariners of dangerous points, shoals, islands, or reefs. Roughly two-thirds of the lights on the Seaway Trail were built at harbor or river entrances, while the remaining lights were erected at more remote, perilous locations. The region's first 11 lights were constructed at ports of entry such as Buffalo and Charlotte, at the mouths of major rivers (Fort Niagara and Tibbetts Point) or at important harbors like Oswego and Sodus Bay. With these and other strategic lights finished, the Lighthouse Service took up the task of protecting ships from peril at more remote locations such as Braddock Point and Thirty Mile Point where lives and fortunes had been lost in several shipwrecks in previous centuries.

The first light to brighten the night skies on the Great Lakes was that at the mouth of the Niagara River where it flows into Lake Ontario. Erected atop the "Castle" at Fort Niagara in about 1781, this light was built in response to the increase in military and commercial traffic precipitated by the Revolutionary War. Nearly forty years would pass before the next light would appear on the Great Lakes, the delay being primarily a by-product of the War of 1812. With the War over however, the federal government went about the business of building lighthouses in earnest. A controversy still exists as to whether the Buffalo, New York, or Presque Isle, Pennsylvania, light was built first (both are circa 1818). By the turn of the next century, more than twenty lighthouses would protect vessels navigating the waterways adjacent to the Seaway Trail.

In 1789, the Congress of the United States recognized the importance of lighting our shores, ensuring that our ships, their crews and cargoes would be safe. Since then, the construction and maintenance of lighthouses has been a federal responsibility. The early lights and their keepers were personally overseen by Presidents

Washington, Adams, and Jefferson; however, as the governing of the country became more complicated, the duty was transferred to the Secretary of the Treasury.

In 1820, lighthouses became the responsibility of the Fifth Auditor of the Treasury, Stephen Pleasonton, a frugal bureaucrat. By 1851, Pleasonton's budget was in order, but the lighthouses, their personnel and general operations were not. Lights in the United States were technologically behind those in Europe where a superior lens had been in use since its perfection in 1822. An in-depth investigation resulted in a complete revamping of the Lighthouse Service and establishment of the Lighthouse Board. Within the next ten years, most working lights in the U.S. were renovated and their towers refitted to accept Fresnel lenses imported from Paris. The Board also established stringent professional standards for lighthouse keepers. America's lighthouses would never again be in such ill-repair nor under such poor management.

A smaller, more manageable Bureau of Lighthouses, consisting of civilians, headed the Lighthouse Service from 1910 to 1939. During this time, lighthouses were converted to electricity, while radio beacons, and electric buoys and fog signals were developed and installed.

The last step in the metamorphosis of the Lighthouse Service occurred in 1939 when the United States Coast Guard assumed responsibility for all aids to navigation. Since that time, the Coast Guard has made technological improvements such as advanced radio techniques and solar-powered beacons.

Over the centuries, lights in the tower lanterns have undergone great change. The first light source was probably a bonfire built on a hillside. With the building of towers, the wood fire was placed on top of the tower, but not without problems as it needed frequent tending and depleted nearby forests. Coal was much preferred by sailors as it burned brighter, but it blackened reflectors quickly and could not be enclosed. The earliest oil lamps, used

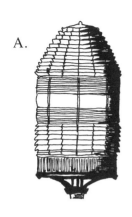

A. *The Fresnel lens developed by Augustin Fresnel in 1822, revolutionized lighthouse illumination and is still used today.*

B. *Vertical section of a fourth order Fresnel lens housed in its lantern with staircase below.*

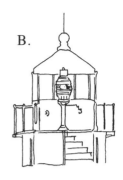

well into the late 1700s, emitted harsh fumes which burned the keepers' eyes and nostrils.

Finally, in 1781, Swiss scientist Ami Argand invented a lamp with a hollow wick allowing oxygen to flow freely, producing a bright, smokeless flame. In 1810 Winslow Lewis convinced the government to use his adaptation of the Argand lamp and parabolic reflector in all the nation's lighthouses. A few years later, French physicist Augustin Fresnel invented a lens system which resembled an enormous hollow beehive around a single lamp (Illus. A.). The light was refracted by prisms at the top and bottom of the lens, creating a single sheet of light which was then magnified many times by a powerful magnifying glass. This method produced a concentrated beam of light visible for several miles. Even today, Fresnel's ingenious lens design is molded into a lighter, plastic version by the U.S.Coast Guard.

The Fifth Auditor had delayed the adoption of the Fresnel lens, due in part to his frugality and in part to his relationship with Lewis, who had a profitable contract with the Lighthouse Service. By the investigation of 1851, only three lights had been equipped with the superior Fresnel lens.

The quest for an efficient fuel was ongoing. The first used in the United States was whale oil. Eventually, only sperm whale oil was used because it burned evenly and brightly. When the price rose, the Lighthouse Board experimented with other fuels such as colza (a wild cabbage derivative), lard oil, kerosene, gasoline, natural gas, fish oil, olive oil, and even porpoise oil. None of these really took hold, however.

Through the years, the main function of the lighthouse keeper was to maintain the brightest light possible. To do this, prior to electricity, he had to keep the oil reservoirs full, the wick trimmed and lit, and the lantern free of smoke. The Argand reflectors, and later the Fresnel lenses also, had to be kept absolutely clean. The lightkeeper's job was one that required long hours and strict discipline. Soon, however, the beginning of the end of this lifestyle would occur.

The first American lighthouse to use electricity was the Statue of Liberty in 1886, but electricity came slowly to other lights. Although tested in 1900 and quickly adopted, many lights had to await generators because they had no power lines. By the 1930s, most lighthouses had been converted. As a lightbulb needs little tending, the elimination of many jobs soon followed. The use of timer switches and multiple bulb holders (which move a new bulb into position when an old one burns out) further reduced the need for the lighthouse keeper.

Today, active lights along the Seaway Trail are either electrically, battery or solar powered. Photovoltaic cells within the solar mechanism generate energy which keep the batteries charged twenty-four hours a day. Keeping the light, a job which once was the basis for an entire lifestyle, and one which often involved whole families, now requires only a routine check every spring and fall.

Although there are no traditional lighthouse keepers left on the Seaway Trail today, a few of the old towers are still active. The lights at Dunkirk, Old Fort Niagara, the Pier Light at Sodus Point, Oswego, and Tibbetts Point are maintained by the United States Coast Guard. The St. Lawrence Seaway Development Corporation keeps the Sunken Rock Light as well as other fixed and floating aids to navigation in the St. Lawrence River, most of which have been converted to solar energy. The present owner of the Barcelona Light faithfully keeps a gas flame glowing nightly in the old stone tower there.

Keepers may no longer live and work at the old structures as they once did, but scattered along the shores of the Seaway Trail are individuals whose fathers or husbands tended the lights here. Many have fascinating stories of terrific storms, shipwrecks and even heroic rescues. They recall being rowed to shore each day to attend school. They tell of often feeling remote and lonely, having no one to play with or talk with for days and weeks. They recall feeling safe and secure within the strong walls of their lighthouse home. Above all, they speak of being thankful to have had such rich experiences and lasting memories.

Come along and enjoy the rich history, varied architecture and panoramic vistas provided by the light towers and keepers dwellings of the Seaway Trail. At Dunkirk, Old Fort Niagara, Charlotte-Genesee, and Old Sodus, lights contain maritime museums and host a variety of special events annually. The three Erie, Pennsylvania, lights have a maritime museum nearby as does the Oswego Lighthouse. Lighthouse grounds, and in some cases interiors, are open to the public. Still others are being preserved by appreciative private owners who now reside in the old, strong, and secure sentinels. Please respect private property.

This 3rd edition of Seaway Trail Lighthouses includes the Presque Isle North Pier Light in Erie, Pennsylvania, with new illustrations for the three lights guarding the 50-mile shoreline along Seaway Trail Pennsylvania. It also updates details on the earlier editions' two dozen lights. We salute the keepers and their families, who patiently and loyally tended the lights, and who risked their own lives to ensure that others would be safe. May their lives and deeds not be forgotten.

BARCELONA LIGHTHOUSE

BARCELONA LIGHTHOUSE
Barcelona, New York
1829

In 1828 Congress designated Portland Harbor (now Barcelona) on Lake Erie as a port of entry and appropriated $5000 for building a lighthouse. One of the oldest structures of its kind on the Great Lakes, the lighthouse and adjacent keeper's dwelling were constructed of a native rough split stone whitewashed "twice over." Standing 40 feet high with a base diameter of 22 feet, the conical tower continues to be an important regional landmark.

Upon completion in May 1829, Joshua Lane, a local clergyman, was selected as its first keeper. Originally illuminated by eleven patent lamps with an equal number of fourteen inch reflectors fueled by oil, the Barcelona Lighthouse would inaugurate the gaslight era two years later with the discovery by local settlers of a nearby "burning spring." Containing natural hydrogen gas and conveyed to the lighthouse through hollowed wooden pipes, this spring would serve as the main energy source for the light for the next nine years. The pipes would occasionally fill with water; therefore it was necessary to use oil for a short time until the water subsided. This pattern continued sporadically until 1838 when the gas spring failed and the lighthouse reverted to oil use exclusively. Although keepers attempted to use the natural gas again, they were unsuccessful. Today, the beacon is lit by gas courtesy of its owner and the Town of Westfield which pays for the gas.

The first public building in the United States to be illuminated by natural gas, the Barcelona Lighthouse was described by one observer as "exceeding both in quantity and brilliancy, anything of the kind I ever saw." Another writer said that "when viewed from the lake at night, the whole tower represented one complete, constant and unwavering blaze."

The keeper's dwelling was originally 32 x 20 feet, as were most structures of its kind and era. Divided into two rooms, with a fireplace in each room, its walls were to be 20" thick. A wing, designated "porch," was attached to the east end of the building and served as the kitchen. The original proposal called for "all inside woodwork to be finished in a plain, decent style, with good seasoned stuff." Over the years the dwelling has been added to, resulting in a picturesque and quaint country cottage (now a private residence).

Decommissioned in 1859 by the Lighthouse Board when it discovered that Barcelona did not possess a harbor, and sold at auction in 1872, the tower and dwelling house remain an excellent example of an early Great Lakes lighthouse. *Please do not trespass* on the property, but enjoy the lighthouse and its keeper's dwelling from the public right of way just a few feet away. They are located on East Lake Road (Route 5) at Barcelona.

DUNKIRK LIGHTHOUSE

DUNKIRK HISTORICAL LIGHTHOUSE
Dunkirk, New York
1826-1875, 1875-present

Situated at Point Gratiot on a bluff overlooking Lake Erie and Dunkirk Harbor, Dunkirk Lighthouse has historically served the dual role of aiding Great Lakes navigation and guiding vessels through the difficult approach to the harbor. In the 1820s, Dunkirk was nearly named the Erie Canal's western terminus; however, when Buffalo instead received the honor, Dunkirk became the chief port city of New York's Southern Tier. The present complex, constructed in 1875, replaced an earlier light commissioned in 1826. Illuminated by a fixed third order Fresnel lens from France, the light is the most prominent on Lake Erie's southern shore with a visibility of seventeen miles.

Architecturally, the red brick keeper's dwelling is an outstanding example of High Victorian Gothic. The facade of the keeper's house is symmetrical with three large but graceful dormers with original wooden braces and finials. Molded and turned braces, boarding and brackets adorn the gable ends of the roof. All the doors and windows have flat stone lintels and sills, and all wooden trim is painted white. The result is a large, strong structure softened and made elegant by its many adornments.

Inside the tower, an ornate, circular, cast-iron stairway winds to the 61-foot lantern with its panoramic view of Lake Erie and Dunkirk Harbor. Originally, the ashlar-pattern tower was cylindrical, but was squared to be more compatible with the keeper's house.

The white bottle-shaped beacon pier light welcoming visitors at the Lighthouse and Veterans Park entrance is one of two such lights on display along the Seaway Trail. Built of boiler plate, they are about 30 feet high and distinguished by four cast-iron port windows and a curved iron door. These typically were equipped with the smallest (sixth order) Fresnel lens and emitted a green or red beam produced by using a colored chimney around the lens.

Deeded to the Dunkirk Historical Lighthouse and Veterans Park Museum, the complex, with gift shop, is open 3rd Monday in April-June/Sept-Oct: M-Tu, Th-Sat, 10 am-2 pm; July-August: M-Tu/Sat, 10 am-4 pm; Nov-Mar: closed. Admission is charged to grounds and 10-room, 3-building museum complex commemorating the lighthouse keeper and the branches of the service with displays of the Coast Guard, Submarine Services, sunken ships and lake freighters. Grounds include the Avenue of Flags. For further information, call 716-366-5050. The Lighthouse is located at 1 Lighthouse Point Drive, off Route 5, in the City of Dunkirk.

BUFFALO MAIN LIGHT

BUFFALO MAIN LIGHTHOUSE
Buffalo, New York
1818, 1833

The Buffalo Main Light marked the gateway to the nation's heartland for the millions of immigrants who settled the interior of the United States. Sited at the mouth of the Buffalo River and Erie Canal, it was seen by settlers as the packet boats approached the wharves at the canal's western terminus. Hundreds of thousands of immigrants ended their journey at these wharves, staying to build and settle the city of Buffalo.

The first Buffalo lighthouse was lighted in 1818, making it and the one at Presque Isle, Pennsylvania, the initial American lighthouses on the Great Lakes. With the dedication of the Erie Canal in 1825, and the subsequent expansion of marine traffic, the inadequacy of the original light became evident. Consequently, a new light was commissioned which would rise above the "smoke of the village." Completed in 1833, the new light rested on top of a 68-foot, octagonal, bluff-colored, limestone tower erected at the end of a 1400-foot pier. An octagonal watchroom with deeply recessed windows rests at the top of a circular stone staircase. Following the investigation of the federal lighthouse system in 1851, many lights received needed facelifts. Buffalo Lighthouse was heightened to 76 feet and fitted with a state of the art Fresnel lens.

Also known locally as "Chinaman's Light" because of the nearby pagoda-like wood tower used to monitor the harbor for illegal Chinese immigrants from Canada, the lighthouse remained in service until 1914. Restored in 1985 and now leased from the U.S. Coast Guard by the Buffalo Lighthouse Association, the tower can best be viewed from the Erie Basin Marina.

The City of Buffalo, United States Coast Guard, and the Buffalo Lighthouse Association are developing parkland at Lighthouse Point to include a 1400-foot riverfront promenade with extensive interpretive signage to increase public access. Other lights can be seen from the Main Light, standing on a breakwater, and from Erie Basin Marina. The ruins of Horseshoe Reef Light are just offshore. On clear days, Canada's Point Abino Light can be seen on the horizon. A restored 1903 breakwater light, nicknamed the "Bottle Light," is displayed near the 1833 tower and has a twin at the entrance to Dunkirk's Lighthouse Park. Farther south along Route 5, the 1903 South Buffalo Light was taken out of service in 1992 and relocated to a navigational aid pole in the same location at the south harbor entrance. North along the Niagara River are three sets of range lights - two of which border the NYS Thruway.

The grounds at the Buffalo Main Light are open daily. The tower is open during waterfront festivals.

BUFFALO INTAKE CRIB LIGHT

**GRAND ISLAND
LIGHTHOUSE**

**NORTH BREAKWATER
SOUTH END LIGHT**

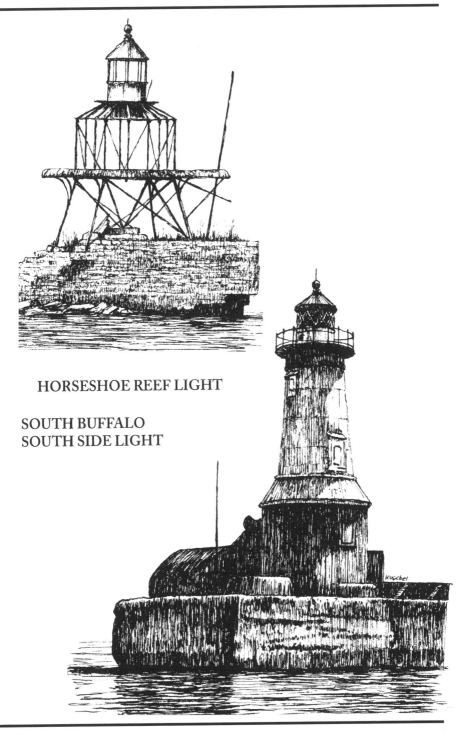

HORSESHOE REEF LIGHT

SOUTH BUFFALO
SOUTH SIDE LIGHT

OLD FORT NIAGARA LIGHTHOUSE

OLD FORT NIAGARA LIGHTHOUSE
Youngstown, New York
1781, 1823, 1872

The Niagara River, joining Lake Ontario and the western Great Lakes, has served as an important harbor and military base of operations since the colonial period. With the increase in military and commercial traffic precipitated by the American Revolution, the need for a navigational aid at the river's mouth became evident. Eventually four lights (including one on the Canadian shore) would be erected at or near Fort Niagara.

The first Fort Niagara Light was established on the roof of the Fort or "Castle" in 1781 or 1782. Probably fueled by whale oil, it was the earliest unofficial lighthouse on the Great Lakes. Next came the Newark Light built in 1804 by the British garrison at Fort George (Fort Mississauga). It survived the intense battles of the War of 1812, but was removed from service in 1814 and not replaced. The U.S. federal government reestablished a light, a squat pedestal and lamp, atop the "Castle" in 1823. The existing stone light went into service in 1872. On the riverbank just south of the fort is the 50' octagonal tower (since extended by an 11' brick watchroom), no longer an active light. The Coast Guard decommissioned it and placed it on an 80 foot tower in May 1993. The Old Fort Niagara Association operates the stone light's base as a museum, gift shop, and information center.

Old Fort Niagara, within Fort Niagara State Park, is a National Historic Landmark. Built by the French in 1726 to monitor the fur trade out of the Great Lakes Basin, it was lost to the British during the French and Indian War, and remained under British control until after the Revolutionary War when it was relinquished to the United States. In 1813, British forces captured the fort once again, fortunately sparing it from destruction. The close of the War of 1812 saw Fort Niagara once again in American hands. Containing the most complete collection of 18th century military architecture in the country, you will here find unique examples of military engineering along with important archeological resources.

Old Fort Niagara holds several annual historic events depicting the French and Indian, Revolutionary, and War of 1812 periods. Regular programming includes soldiers on duty, musket firing, 18th century cooking and barracks life, and Old Fort Niagara Guard with drills, muskets and cannon firings. The fort is open year'round. The lighthouse exhibit and gift shop are open June weekends, daily July 1-Labor Day. To reach the light from Niagara Falls, follow Robert Moses Parkway North; from Rochester and points east, follow Route 18 West to Robert Moses Parkway South. For more information, call 716-745-7611 or check www.oldfortniagara.org.

THIRTY MILE POINT LIGHTHOUSE

THIRTY MILE POINT LIGHTHOUSE
Barker, New York
1875

Thirty Mile Point Lighthouse was erected in 1875 along Lake Ontario's shoreline near the mouth of Golden Hill Creek. It derived its name from being located 30 miles east of the Niagara River. The site was selected to warn vessels of a treacherous sandbar and dangerous shoal where several vessels had been shipwrecked in the prior two centuries. Perhaps the largest of the ill-fated ships was the English naval frigate, *H.M.S. Ontario*, which sank on Halloween night 1780. Eighty-eight passengers including the retired commander of Fort Niagara lost their lives. Reputedly, $15,000 in gold and silver was lost in the disaster.

The *Mary* went down at Thirty Mile Point in 1817. Around 1834, Daniel Cartwright, a local farmer who pastured his cattle near the creek, observed several sailors row up the creek and excavate a chest before returning to their ship. Mr. Cartwright felt it may have been a chest of gold buried by survivors of the *Mary*. Despite these interesting stories, the actual name "Golden Hill," shown on early French maps, was probably related to blooming goldenrod on the former offshore island at the creek mouth.

Thirty Mile Point Lighthouse is constructed of hand-carved limestone transported by schooner from Chaumont Bay at Lake Ontario's eastern end. Seventy feet high, with a circular steel stairway, the tower offers a panoramic view across the lake to Canada. The beam from its 2000 pound, third order Fresnel lens could be seen from a distance of 16 miles. Eventually, the keeper's house was converted to accommodate two families. Each keeper had a very busy 24-hour shift.

In 1935, the U.S. Coast Guard assumed ownership and maintained the light for several years. The need for the light ended with the erosion of the sandbar. On December 17, 1958, the light was dismantled and the lighthouse doors closed. A simple steel skeleton structure was erected nearby to replace the once imposing Thirty Mile Point Lighthouse.

A light returned to service in the lighthouse in 1997 is now a navigational light operated by the Friends of 30 Mile Point Lighthouse. The lighthouse is the property of New York State on the grounds of Golden Hill State Park. The old horse stable is now a garage; the fog horn building is a camper recreation hall. Nearby are 50 campsites, a picnic shelter and marina with boat launch. One of several nature trails begins at the lighthouse and leads to the mouth of Golden Hill Creek. You may tour the lighthouse for free Memorial Day-Labor Day Fri-Sun/holidays, 2-4 pm. A self-guided tour is also available. For details, call 716-795-3885, off-season: 716-795-3117. The lighthouse is located on Lower Lake Road in the Town of Somerset, Barker, NY. From Route 18, go north on Route 269, west on Lower Lake Road. Use campsite park entrance.

BRADDOCK POINT LIGHTHOUSE

BRADDOCK POINT LIGHTHOUSE
Hilton, New York
1896

Conceived by the Lighthouse Board in the last decade of the 19th century to be the brightest beacon on Lake Ontario, the Braddock Point Lighthouse is actually sited on Bogus Point, three miles to the west. Architect Lt. Col. Jared A. Smith based his design on the 1829 Cleveland Light which was torn down in 1895 and whose ornate brass lantern, Fresnel lens from France, and metal work were used to complete the Braddock Light.

Completed in 1896, the complex included the Victorian keeper's house and the 110 foot red brick octagonal tower. Keepers of Braddock Point Light climbed the tower's 118 circular steps at least twice a day to maintain the "brightest light on Lake Ontario." The third-and-a-half order lens transmitted a powerful 20,000 candlepower beam visible some eighteen miles out on the Lake—its white light guiding passing ships eastward to Rochester or west toward the Welland Canal and upper Great Lakes.

Following continuous operation for 57 years, Braddock Point Light was extinguished on January 1, 1954. Shortly thereafter the U.S. Coast Guard removed the upper two-thirds of the tower due to extensive structural damage. In the absence of full-time keepers, duck hunters and trespassers used and misused the sentinel, knocking out windows and exposing the structure to the harsh elements. Soon, the house was full of debris and in ill-repair.

Purchased by an enthusiastic couple in 1957 for a summer home, the light was given a new lease on life. In 1986 the house changed hands again. The present owners restored the house to its original beauty. Structural walls which had been removed were replaced, details from the original drawings now adorn each room. Even the grounds have been restored. The tower was rebuilt in 1995 to a height of 65 feet. The U.S. Coast Guard relit the light February 28, 1996. It can be seen for a distance of 13 nautical miles in clear visibility.

Please do not trespass on the present owner's property, but view the stately structure from the road. Braddock Point Lighthouse is located at the end of Lighthouse Road off the Lake Ontario State Parkway (Seaway Trail) just west of Braddock Bay.

CHARLOTTE-GENESEE LIGHTHOUSE

CHARLOTTE-GENESEE LIGHTHOUSE
Rochester, New York
1821, 1863

As commercial marine traffic increased on Lake Ontario in the 19th century, the lighting of entryways at key ports became necessary. In 1805, Congress established the Port of Genesee and a collector was appointed for the new customs district. Since the port was surrounded by marshlands and the river partially blocked by a sandbar, a lighthouse was essential, particularly with the advent of the steamboat. Thus, in 1821 the United States Government purchased 3 1/4 acres of land from Mehitabel Hincher, whose husband had built a log cabin on the site in 1792.

Erected on a bluff overlooking the mouth of the Genesee River and Port of Rochester, the lighthouse stands in an area known as Charlotte, formerly a village separate from the city of Rochester. Shifting sandbars made it difficult for captains to find a safe entrance to the river; in 1829, the first piers were built to control the problem. Wind and wave action redistributed the sand, creating a beach at the base of the bluff. As the years wore on, the piers had to be lengthened and the beach grew, causing the lighthouse to be somewhat removed from the water's edge.

The 40-foot octagonal tower is made of Medina Sandstone. The typically austere keeper's residence was replaced in 1863 by the present brick structure. In 1881 the Lighthouse Board removed the light from service, although the residence continued to be used by Lighthouse Service personnel. A civilian keeper was housed here until 1940, when the property was transferred to the U.S. Coast Guard which provided minimal maintenance of the keeper's house until 1982.

In the mid-60s, plans were made to tear down the tower, considered surplus government property and deemed useless. It was saved, primarily through the efforts of Charlotte High School students. It seems the architect used the lighthouse as inspiration for the design of their school, and they weren't about to lose the landmark so much a part of their lives. A successful letter writing campaign saved the lighthouse from destruction.

The complex, now owned by Monroe County, is leased to the Charlotte-Genesee Lighthouse Historical Society, which opens the tower and dwelling to the public on weekends, with daily access to the lighthouse grounds, and special tours by appointment year'round. Its enthusiastic personnel maintain a museum and gift shop inside the keeper's house and a Native American and geological display in an outbuilding annex. From the east, take Lake Shore Blvd (Seaway Trail) to Lake Avenue, north to Holy Cross Church. From the west, take Lake Ontario State Parkway to its end, turn left on Lake Ave., proceed to Holy Cross Church. Lighthouse and parking lot are behind the church.

OLD SODUS LIGHTHOUSE

OLD SODUS LIGHTHOUSE
Sodus Point, New York
1825, 1870-71

In 1824, local residents and lake captains united to establish a lighthouse on Great Sodus Bay. Their successful petition to Congress resulted in the construction of a rough split stone tower and keeper's dwelling in 1825. It was replaced by the existing lighthouse in 1870 when the need for extensive repairs was recognized. Limestone for the 45-foot tower and attached 2 1/2 story dwelling was quarried in Kingston, Ontario. Stone from the original lighthouse was used to construct a protective jetty. The tower was fitted with a fourth order Fresnel lens.

In 1834, the first piers were erected at the entrance to the bay and a beacon placed at the end. A permanent beacon was installed in 1870 in conjunction with construction of the replacement lighthouse. In 1901, the Lighthouse Board determined that this beacon was sufficient and decommissioned the on-shore lighthouse light. The Coast Guard used the keeper's house until the mid-1960s. The Coast Guard turned the historic lighthouse over to the Town of Sodus in 1984. Today, Old Sodus Lighthouse, on both the State and National Historic Registers, is leased and maintained by the Sodus Bay Historical Society.

The climb to the lantern room is well worth the trip for a clear view of the spectacular Chimney Bluffs and of Sodus Bay and Lake Ontario, often dotted with sailboats. The downstairs museum exhibits sailing, shipping, and lighthouse artifacts and exhibits of life and activities around Sodus Bay. Chamberlain Library, on the 2nd floor, is a small reference library open to the public. A 1st floor gift shop offers a variety of gifts and lighthouse memorabilia.

The museum is open May 1-Oct 31, Tues-Sun, 10-5. Group tours are welcome anytime with prior arrangement. Donations are gratefully accepted. Summer events include concerts July 4th—Labor Day weekend Sunday. To reach the lighthouse, take Route 104 to Route 14 north into the Village of Sodus Point, turn right at the 4-way stop, go 1 block to Ontario Street, turn left and drive to the end. For more information, call 315-483-4936.

OSWEGO WEST PIERHEAD LIGHTHOUSE

OSWEGO WEST PIERHEAD LIGHTHOUSE
Oswego, New York
1822, 1836, 1934

The first lighthouse at Oswego (1822) was sited on the grounds of Fort Ontario on the east shore of the Oswego River. The keeper's residence, typically sparse in form and function, can still be seen at the fort, a New York State Historic Site open to the public.

The original light was replaced in 1836 by a light on the west pier. This second light was octagonal, built of gray stone with an attached oil room. Its fixed white third order lens could be seen for 15 miles on Lake Ontario. In service until 1930, this light saw much economic growth in the port city of Oswego. Although it was torn down in 1930, the light and Oswego Harbor are still seen in their 19th century glory in an impressive mural in the Oswego City Savings Bank on West First Street.

The present lighthouse was erected in 1934, at the end of the new stone west pier. It consists of a square white metal building with a red pyramidal roof and attached tower. The rotating fourth order Fresnel lens was tinted with red panels on the lantern windows, thus giving the powerful beam its characteristic color until 1995 when the Coast Guard removed the lens and replaced it with a new "VRB-25 Lantern." The light is now solar-powered using 15 to 35-watt solar panels; its flashing characteristic was changed to an alternating white and red 10-second flash. The red-tinted windows were removed and clear glass put in place.

Several Coast Guardsmen were killed here in a 1942 boating accident while changing keepers. Shortly thereafter, the Oswego Light was automated and remains in use today. Considered a fine example of modern lighthouse architecture, the structure is currently owned and maintained by the U.S. Coast Guard Station at Oswego.

Bisecting the City of Oswego, the Oswego Canal provides an important linkage to the Erie Barge Canal system. From the port of Oswego, the recreational boater has access to the Great Lakes, the St. Lawrence River, the Mohawk and Hudson Rivers, and the Champlain Canal. Other attractions within the city which relate to the area's maritime history include three working locks on the Canal, the Harborwalk, and the H. Lee White Marine Museum. The museum is home to the Fresnel lens which was removed from the light in 1995.

Although the lighthouse is not accessible to the public, a very pleasant vantage point is from Oswego's Breitbeck Park. From the Seaway Trail (Route 104/Bridge Street), turn on West First Street toward the lake. Make a left on VanBuren and quickly bear right onto Lake Street. The park, just past Wright's Landing, has benches which overlook the marina and lighthouse.

SELKIRK LIGHTHOUSE

SELKIRK LIGHTHOUSE
Port Ontario, New York
1838

Selkirk Lighthouse, at the mouth of the Salmon River and Lake Ontario, is unique in structure and appearance among all the Seaway Trail lights. Its "birdcage" lantern—a hexagonal dome of small-paned glass, wrought iron and beaten copper plate—predates those constructed to house the later Fresnel lens. Apparently only four such lanterns remain in the U.S., of which this and only one other are serviceable.

Had the light not been decommissioned in 1858, the lantern would have been rebuilt to better serve the 6th order Fresnel lens it held during its last years of official service. The lighthouse and its original lantern are a unique monument to the design of Winslow Lewis and to spartan functionality. Retirement also froze in time one of the last remaining wooden lantern room decks and the original hand-cut wooden spiral staircase leading to it.

Citizens and speculators, anticipating construction of a major port, purchased lots in nearby Port Ontario and along the Salmon River in 1836-37. While surveying, a government engineer determined the lower river could provide safe anchorage for 30 commercial vessels and recommended harbor development. As a sign encouraging prospective growth, the federal government ordered Selkirk Lighthouse built in 1837. Construction of a railway through nearby Pulaski in the early 1840s, and an Erie Canal spur into the Oswego River, thence to Lake Ontario, diverted the hoped-for development. The little port nevertheless served a modest shipbuilding industry, fishing fleet, and declining commercial & passenger service into the early 1900s until harbor siltation allowed passage of only shallow-draft fishing and pleasure craft. A Federal Harbor of Refuge, constructed here in 1987, occasionally sees 100+ foot vessels.

One tale claims the light was named for sailor and Robinson Crusoe model Alexander Selkirk, abandoned on a South Sea island in 1704 for having disobeyed his captain. Most likely, the light and surrounding hamlet were named for Thomas Douglas, Earl of Selkirk, who first purchased land along the Salmon River's north shore. Lucius B. Cole, the longest apparent keeper here (1852-1890), kept the light, although officially inactive, until his death. A local paper reported that his mother was President James Monroe's sister Olive and hinted at nepotism.

Selkirk Light, placed on the National Register in 1970, was officially relit in 1989. Privately-owned, it is one of the world's few lights open for overnight accommodations. It is located at the west end of Lake Road (Co Rt 5), a mile west of Rt 3 (Seaway Trail) in Port Ontario. For reservations and information, call 315-298-6688 or visit http://www.maine.com/lights/.

STONY POINT LIGHTHOUSE

LIGHTHOUSES of the GOLDEN CRESCENT

Five Seaway Trail lighthouses serve as sentinels for Jefferson County's Golden Crescent, a region of beautiful embayments and secluded harbors, characterized by islands and peninsulas which project well into Lake Ontario's eastern basin. Steeped in the nation's history, it lies south of the St. Lawrence River and Canada.

STONY POINT
Henderson Harbor, New York
1830, 1869

Immediately east of Galloo and Stony Islands lies Stony Point, an anvil-like peninsula which, with the mainland, shapes Henderson Bay and Harbor. This beautiful harbor's sunsets are consistently breathtaking, the entire area being a photographer's dream. Stony Point Light, erected in 1869, is similar in design to that on Horse Island, consisting of a 50-foot square tower with an attached keeper's dwelling. This light replaced an 1830 lighthouse whose foundation still remains. Removed from service in 1945, the light is now a privately owned residence on Lighthouse Road in the picturesque town of Henderson Harbor. To see the Lighthouse, take Route 3 (Seaway Trail) to Military Road on the south side of the harbor, to Lighthouse Road. This light is privately-owned, but you are welcome to enjoy the view and take photographs.

GALLOO ISLAND
Off Henderson Harbor, New York
1820, 1867

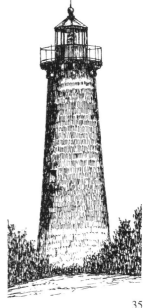

Galloo (also spelled Galoo) Island Light in Lake Ontario west of Henderson Harbor was first established in 1820. The present lighthouse erected in 1867. Four bids were submitted in Fall 2000 to acquire the light, listed on the National Register of Historic Places, through government auction. The sale included a 55' limestone tower, brick fog signal building, cast iron oil house, and a 1 1/2-story keeper's dwelling in poor condition on one-acre of land on the privately-owned Galloo Island. The U.S. Coast Guard will continue to maintain a navigation beacon on site, but not in the lighthouse.

HORSE ISLAND LIGHTHOUSE

HORSE ISLAND LIGHTHOUSE
Sackets Harbor, New York
1870

Horse Island lies at the entrance to Sackets Harbor, the nation's most important shipbuilding center during the War of 1812. Headquarters for the U.S. Navy on the Great Lakes, Sackets Harbor was home to the thousands of shipwrights, carpenters, sailors and soldiers gathered to construct, sail, and defend the fleet. During the war, one third of the United States Army and a quarter of the Navy were stationed at Sackets Harbor.

Horse Island was the site of two battles during the war. The Albany Volunteers established "Camp Volunteer" on Horse Island, 300 yards from the mainland, because Colonel Alexander Macomb was convinced it was the place the British would strike first. During the night of May 28th, General Jacob Brown, commanding the militia, visited Horse Island and ordered the Volunteers to retreat to the mainland as soon as an attack began. Sackets Harbor was successfully defended by the first U.S. Light Dragoons under Colonel Electus Backus and General Brown's militia and continued to serve a critical role until the war's end.

The harbor's importance as a shipbuilding, military and commercial center continued well into the 19th century. The first American Great Lakes steamship, *Ontario*, was constructed at the shipworks here. Connected to New York State's interior by military and public turnpikes, the Black River Canal system and the railroad, Sackets Harbor served as the principal shipping point for the region's lumber, agricultural and manufacturing industries.

Horse Island Lighthouse was erected in 1870. Constructed of native brick and since painted, the structure and 28 acre island on which it stands are now privately owned. Architecturally related to the Stony Point Lighthouse, it is accessible only by boat and is not open to the public. The tower and attached keeper's dwelling are visible from the Sackets Harbor Historic Battlefield which is open May-Sept and to groups by appointment.

Today, the village of Sackets Harbor is enjoying an unprecedented renaissance with three historic districts: downtown, Sackets Harbor Battlefield State Historic Site, and Madison Barracks. Downtown features a Lake Ontario view, restaurants, shops, museums, and the Seaway Trail Discovery Center. Special events feature tall ships, fireworks, and summer Sunday concerts on the waterfront. Madison Barracks, which encompasses Forts Volunteer and Pike and was maintained as an active Army post until the end of WWII, is a residential resort area. Sackets Harbor (with Buffalo and Rochester) is one of three New York State Heritage Areas on the Seaway Trail.

TIBBETTS POINT LIGHTHOUSE

TIBBETTS POINT LIGHTHOUSE
Cape Vincent, New York
1827, 1854

Tibbetts Point Light marks the entrance into the St. Lawrence River. Once part of a 600 acre parcel patented to Capt. John Tibbett, the three-acre lighthouse site was deeded to the U.S. Government which erected a lighthouse here in 1827. Fueled by whale oil, this light remained in service until the construction of the present tower in 1854. This 69 foot white conical stucco tower contained a 50 candlepower oil lamp of fixed beam and was equipped with a fourth order Fresnel lens. Later, the oil lamps were changed to a 500 watt, 15,000 candlepower light with the lens remaining.

The steam-operated fog whistle was added in 1896. In 1927, it was replaced by an air diaphone powered by a diesel engine with the blasts automatically timed. The whistle and air diaphone were replaced by a radio beacon which guides ships into the river.

The lighthouse complex consists of the tower, a two-story residence (1800), steam fog signal building, a one-story brick building housing two air compressors (1927), and an iron oil house. A Coast Guard Station until May 1981, the keeper's dwelling is now an American Youth Hostel. In 1988, the Tibbetts Point Lighthouse Society formed for the purpose of restoring the lighthouse and grounds as an educational and historic entity. The tower, a State Historic Site, is still an active light maintained by the Coast Guard. It has a fourth order Fresnel lens, but is on the list to receive a new VRB-25 lantern. This will increase the light's range from 16 to 22 miles. At present, this lighthouse has the only classical Fresnel lens still in operation on Lake Ontario.

In 1993 a new Visitors Center and Lighthouse Museum became a popular tourist destination. Museum and grounds with picnic tables and a Seacoast 20x viewing telescope are open Memorial Day—September weekends, daily July-August. An overnight hostel is open May 15-Oct 15, call 315-654-3450. The Lighthouse, Visitors Center, and Hostel are located at the end of Tibbetts Point Road (County Rt. 6), Cape Vincent, NY, 315-654-2700.

* * * * * * * *

A smaller, square, masonry lighthouse welcomes visitors approaching Cape Vincent from the south on Route 12E. One of two such lights originally erected at each end of the village breakwall, it was built in the first decade of the 20th century.

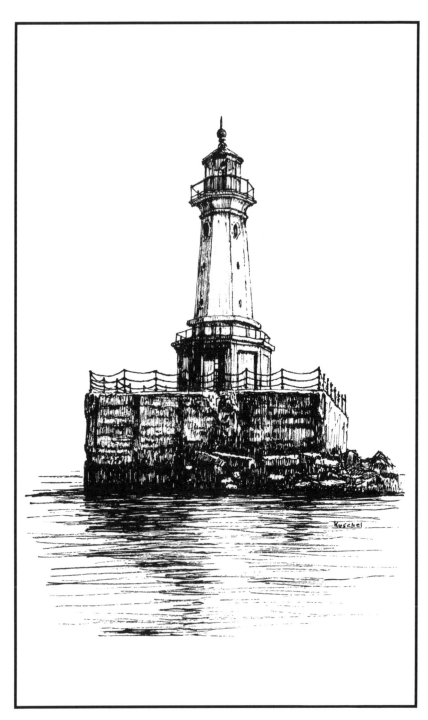

EAST CHARITY SHOAL LIGHTHOUSE

EAST CHARITY SHOAL LIGHTHOUSE
Off Cape Vincent, New York
Rebuilt on Lake Ontario, 1929

In 1929 the 35 foot lighthouse leaning toward the waters off the Lake Erie shore near Vermilion, Ohio, disappeared. It was a white, cast iron lighthouse with a wide, red stripe. U.S. Coast Guard and Army Corps of Engineer records showed that it was sent to Buffalo. It was speculated that its cast iron was sold for scrap. An 18 foot skeleton tower replaced it.

Vermilion residents, led by Ted Wakefield who had played in the lighthouse as a boy, searched without success to locate the Vermilion Light. Wakefield helped raise funds for a $67,000 replica to be built near the home where he grew up. He later donated that home now housing the Inland Seas Maritime Museum of the Great Lakes Historical Society. Wakefield died in 1992 after 60 years of searching.

In September 1994, trying to answer his grandchildren's questions about their ancestors, Olin M. Stevens of Columbus, Ohio, opened an old trunk. Inside a newspaper story told of his grandfather's first Lake Ontario lighthouse assignment at Tibbetts Point Lighthouse in Cape Vincent, New York. It mentioned the nearby East Charity Shoal Light which was formerly his charge at Vermilion, Ohio. Olin W. Stevens, a third-generation lighthouse keeper, had arrived in Cape Vincent in 1937.

While visiting the Great Lakes museum seeking more information about his grandfather, Olin M. Stevens learned of the search for the Vermilion light and mentioned the old newspaper article. The missing lighthouse had been found. The white lighthouse stands on the rocky shoal on a 10 foot black base with a 12 foot concrete platform below that. A five foot section, perhaps patching an entrance area, was added to the light when it was rebuilt on Lake Ontario in 1929. The light still operates as a reference point for ships navigating the St. Lawrence Seaway channel. East Charity Shoal Lighthouse is located seven miles off the Cape Vincent, New York, shoreline. A Seacoast 20x viewing telescope was installed in 1997 in memory of W. Howard Smith at the Tibbetts Point Lighthouse, Cape Vincent. Visitors can now see East Charity Shoal Lighthouse at a distance.

ROCK ISLAND LIGHTHOUSE

ROCK ISLAND LIGHTHOUSE
Off Fisher's Landing, New York
1847, 1882

One of several lighthouses erected on the St. Lawrence River, the Rock Island Light is the only one that retains the tower and all its auxiliary structures. Constructed in 1882, the lighthouse replaced the combination lighthouse/keeper's house of 1847. The fieldstone smokehouse is the only structure to have survived from the earlier period. These two buildings, along with the generator house (1900), boathouse (1920), carpenter's shop (1882), and the Shingle Style keeper's house (1882) represents a microcosm of the river's maritime life during the late 19th and early 20th centuries.

Frank Ward was the last keeper at Rock Island Light. He and his family were stationed here from 1939-1941, when they were transferred to shore to conserve money during WWII. Ward had several battery operated lights with generators to tend. His widow, Sally, of Clayton, recounted numerous incidents which occurred during their tenure at Rock Island Light, as well as at Crossover Island, where they were previously stationed. A frantic woman once came to their door wanting him to locate her husband, a local fisherman who had failed to return home after a day on the river. Mr. Ward was able to find him, stranded on an island after his boat had been swept away by the wake of a large ship passing by. This apparently was quite a common occurrence. On another occasion, Ward helped save the life of a man whose companion had drowned. In a sick bed for several weeks as a result of this incident, Mr. Ward never fully regained his health.

Today, in the ownership of New York State, Rock Island Light is maintained as a park by the Thousand Islands Region of the Office of Parks, Recreation & Historic Preservation. A citizen's interest group has raised and donated funds to help maintain the site. Volunteers manicure the lawn, plant flowers, paint the lower half of the tower, and generally keep a watchful and loving eye on the property.

The public is free to wander around or picnic on the island during daylight hours. There is minimal docking and you should expect to "tie off." From the U.S. mainland, the complex is visible from the quaint hamlet of Fishers Landing, off Route 12 at Route 180 just a few miles southwest of the 1000 Islands International Bridge. It can also be seen from the picturesque community of Thousand Island Park on Wellesley Island.

SUNKEN ROCK LIGHTHOUSE

SUNKEN ROCK LIGHTHOUSE
Off Alexandria Bay, New York
1847

Located on Bush Island, the octagonal brick light tower marks the east entrance to the narrows between Wellesley Island and the mainland. Constructed in 1847 and refitted in 1855, the tower is now sheathed with a steel cone-shaped cover. In an especially picturesque setting, it provides the easterly frame for a vista which encompasses Heart Island and Boldt Castle, the George Boldt Yacht House (on the National Register and newly reopened in 1997), and the Tennis Island and Thousand Island Club complexes on Wellesley Island.

Still in active service, it is owned by the Saint Lawrence Seaway Development Corporation. Converted in 1988 to solar energy, the panels of photovoltaic cells generate and store the sun's energy during daylight hours for use during periods of darkness and reduced visibility. Some 100 fixed and 133 floating aids were converted to this system by 1990.

The narrows immediately upstream from the Sunken Rock Light were the site of one of the most recent and spectacular shipwrecks within the Great Lakes/St. Lawrence Seaway System. On November 20, 1974, the 640-foot *Roy A. Jodrey* struck Pullman Shoal off the village of Alexandria Bay. Laden with more than twenty tons of iron pellets, the ship remained afloat some four hours before capsizing and slipping beneath the surface. Remaining on the bottom to this day, it presents no hazard to shipping as the water depth is estimated at approximately 250 feet.

Max Walts of Alexandria Bay is the son of the last keeper at Sunken Rock. He often assisted his father, Horace, as he performed his duties at the light, including many routine responsibilities completed on a daily, weekly and seasonal basis. In the early days, they rowed to the island in a St. Lawrence skiff to tend the light. Each morning, after extinguishing and cleaning the light, he covered the costly Fresnel lens with white linen to prevent the formation of bubbles in the glass, then went about the business of maintaining the rest of the tower. Each spring, a Mr. House, from Buffalo, arrived to take orders for supplies. Mr. Walts, then responsible for both Sunken Rock and Sisters Island, ordered everything the two lights would need—brooms, mops, brass polish, paint, etc. He mixed his own paints and hand made each battery from ingredients he ordered.

The performance of keepers was regularly evaluated, the very best receiving a star to keep for a year signifying excellence. Horace Walts was a recipient of this award for nine consecutive years, ultimately being presented with a permanent gold star with a diamond at its center.

You may view Sunken Rock and its scenic backdrop from the waterfront in downtown Alexandria Bay.

SISTERS ISLAND LIGHTHOUSE

SISTERS ISLAND LIGHTHOUSE
Off Chippewa Bay, New York
1870

The native limestone lighthouse on Three Sisters Island was constructed circa 1870 to mark a difficult channel on the Canadian side of the island. Attached to the rear of the 2 1/2 story keeper's house, the square tower rises about 60 feet. Its gables feature framing supports in the Stick Style of architecture typical of that era. The only structure on Three Sisters Island, save for a small shed, the lighthouse is in excellent condition. Two dormer windows on the front and a slate roof give the house added charm, as do deep window seats and large interior rooms.

Interestingly, with the commissioning of the lighthouse, the river channel was relocated to the American side of the island. This entailed the blasting of the bedrock at the river bottom. An extremely hazardous operation, the charges were placed into drilled holes by divers who worked from a support barge. During a summer thunder and lightning storm, the dynamite on the barge exploded and killed nine crew members. In an unrelated incident, a coal-laden ship strayed from the main channel striking Upper Brothers Island. Its wreckage remains on the river bottom.

Horace Walts tended Sisters Island while it was fueled by oil and later by gas. A local phenomenon which greatly annoyed him was the annual invasion of the shadfly. These fleshy insects populate the Hammond-Ogdensburg region in numbers great enough to cover the ground. At Sisters Island, they would occasionally block the oxygen intake and extinguish the flame, causing a dangerous gas leak within the tower; during this time, the keeper had to maintain a constant watch on the flame.

The privately owned Sisters Island Light cannot be seen from the American mainland. The hiring of a boat and guide from Alexandria Bay or Chippewa Bay is well worth the expense, however. Perhaps you'd like to combine the jaunt with a fishing or hunting trip; the adjacent shoals provide habitat for a wide variety of fish and waterfowl species.

Nearby is Dark Island, so named because of dense evergreens which prevented the sun from penetrating to the surface. The Chippewas, who named the region Manatonana (Garden of the Great Spirit), once used the rounded holes in the island's bedrock for their cookfires. About 1900, Frederick C. Bourne, head of the Singer Sewing Company, bought the island and built Jorstadt Castle, rivaling Boldt Castle and castles along the Rhine. Made of granite from nearby Oak Island, the castle and its towers are truly magnificent. Stone boathouses, a pavilion, tennis and squash courts, retaining walls and wooded walks complete the island. Now owned by the Harold Martin Evangelistic Association, Inc., it is the site of religious conferences and retreats.

CROSSOVER ISLAND LIGHTHOUSE

CROSSOVER ISLAND LIGHTHOUSE
Off Chippewa Bay, New York
1848, 1882

Crossover Island Lighthouse, constructed in 1848, was so named for the point where ships crossed between the American and the Canadian Channels. Rebuilt in 1882 because inferior materials had originally been used, the keeper's residence was modeled after Tibbetts Point. The lighthouse complex consisted of a six-room residence, a steel tower with 6th order Fresnel lens, a hen house, barn, privy, and oil and ash houses.

Daniel Hill, a career keeper for the Lighthouse Service, served at Buffalo Reef, Thirty Mile Point, Ogdensburg, and Huron lights, and at Crossover Light from 1909 to 1931. He kept detailed logs. During his career, he rescued more than 400 stranded mariners, the most dramatic occurring when a small biplane crashed just off the island. As the three passengers were safely brought ashore, the plane exploded and burned. In the *Thousand Island Sun* and two books now out of print, Daniel's son, Ralph of Kenmore, NY, coupled childhood memories of Crossover with his father's logs to publish many fascinating stories about the keeper's life and family there.

Rowed by their father across the 3/4-mile channel in a St. Lawrence skiff, the keeper's four children attended a one-room schoolhouse on the mainland. The ash house doubled as a smokehouse where his wife smoked hams, fish and eels. Particularly coveted treats were the smoked eels, packed in jars for neighbors and visitors to savor on special occasions.

In June of each year, eel flies hatch, mate, lay their eggs and die—all within 48 hours. Millions collect in a narrow strip off the island, attracting eels to the surface to feed. The Hill family harvested up to 200 eels nightly, skinning and cleaning them for smoking the next morning.

The river lighthouses were served by the *S.S. Crocus*, a supply ship and buoy tender. Home to the District Superintendent from April until mid-December, the ship and its crew placed navigational aids and channel markings each year. The *Crocus* also served as a base for lighthouse construction work. Each lighthouse was inspected semiannually for conformity to Board standards. The inspections were thorough—even under beds and in closets. Supplies were delivered at this time, consisting primarily of coal, kerosene oil, soap, paint, etc. Also left would be a large box of books, the previous year's to be delivered to the next station.

Today the light is no longer in service, replaced by a nearby skeleton light. The island is privately owned, as a summer residence. The owners are delighted to own both of Ralph Hill's publications and to have corresponded with him. Visible from the Route 12 scenic overlook east of Chippewa Bay, the light provides a striking foreground element in the panoramic view of the eastern 1000 Islands region of the Seaway Trail.

OGDENSBURG HARBOR LIGHTHOUSE

OGDENSBURG HARBOR LIGHTHOUSE
Ogdensburg, New York
1834, 1900

This light, erected in 1900, is the second to occupy this low rocky point at the confluence of the Oswegatchie and St. Lawrence Rivers. The original lighthouse, which dated to 1834, was refitted in 1870. The existing lighthouse, a substantial cut stone structure 1 1/2 stories high, includes an attached 65 foot tower. Lighthouse Point, in addition to containing the Harbor Lighthouse, has also been the site of Fort La Presentation and a "pest house" for cholera victims.

Francis Piquet, a French missionary, established a mission fort at the mouth of the River La Presentation (Oswegatchie) in 1749. The decision to place the mission at this site was influenced by the emigration to French Canada of a significant number of Indians and in recognition that the fort would control passage on the St. Lawrence between the Great Lakes and Montreal. The mission would be the first permanent settlement in northern New York State.

Fort La Presentation was constructed of vertical log pickets and a small house which served as a bastion. In 1749, a band of Mohawk Indians, perhaps on the orders of Sir William Johnson, burned the fort and two vessels anchored offshore. Following this incident a detachment of 10 soldiers was dispatched from Montreal to secure the mission. At its peak, perhaps 100 Iroquois lived at the fort, cultivating vegetables and raising chickens and livestock. An archeological investigation ascertained the fort's boundaries and collected period artifacts. A local group is now campaigning to "rebuild" the fort as an educational and tourist attraction.

Immediately east of the lighthouse on the east bank of the Oswegatchie stands the United States Customs House, the oldest federal building in active use in the U.S.. Built in 1810 by Joseph Rosseel as a store and warehouse, it has withstood the ravages of two wars. During the War of 1812, the city was captured by the British with the battle fought at and around the store, and during the Civil War it housed the Massachusetts Company of Union Troops engaged in protecting the northern border against raids by Confederate partisans. Both the lighthouse and Customs House are listed on the National Register of Historic Places.

One block further east is the Frederic Remington Museum, filled with paintings, bronzes, and memorabilia of this famous artist. Renowned primarily for his Western art, Remington resided in Ogdensburg for a time, and many of his paintings are of the St. Lawrence River region and the Adirondack Mountains to the south.

The lighthouse, now privately owned, is open upon request at the owner's convenience. It is located at 1 Jackson Street, Ogdensburg.

LAND LIGHTHOUSE, ERIE, PA

LAND LIGHTHOUSE
Erie, PA - Seaway Trail Pennsylvania
1818, 1867

The Land Lighthouse, first built in 1818 and reconstructed several times, overlooks the entrance to the channel leading into the Erie Harbor from the east. Its location on the mainland gave it the advantage of additional elevation on the bank above water level, allowing incoming vessels to home in on the channel entrance.

Recently restored, this light guided ships into the channel between lake and harbor for 80 years. It is the third consecutive lighthouse tower at this site.

Now known as the Land Lighthouse, it was first officially known as the Presque Isle Light Station and later as the Erie Light Station. The first structure, completed in 1818, lays claim to being the first lighthouse on the Great Lakes. It was 20 feet high and consisted of multiple oil lamps. Eventually, structural instability led to a 56-foot high replacement tower in 1858, with a single lamp magnified by a lens system. A lighthouse keeper's house was also built.

Structural instability again required replacement and in 1867 a third, 49-foot, sandstone tower was built on top of a massive foundation. This one operated until 1880, when the federal government ordered it closed. For the next five years the approach to the harbor was illuminated by peninsula-based lighthouses, while the Land Lighthouse was reconditioned, reopening in 1885 for a final 14 years.

In 1899 the restored third lighthouse cast its last light. The property remained federal until 1934 when it was transferred to the City of Erie as a park, complete with the nonfunctional lighthouse. A lens similar to the 3rd order Fresnel lens removed from the Land Lighthouse in 1901 can be seen at the Erie County Historical Society at 419 State Street, Erie. The Erie Maritime Museum at 150 E. Front Street, Erie, has the lens which dates back to the 1890s and was removed from the Presque Isle North Pier Light ten years ago. Call ahead to 814-452-2744 to ask to see this light which is not yet on display.

The Erie Land Lighthouse, on the National Register of Historic Places, is located off E. 6th Street on Lighthouse Street. A grant has been secured to replace the light's top section and to add the light to maps as a secondary navigation tool. Ferry docks for boats traveling to and from Canada are also planned.

For more information, contact the Seaway Trail Pennsylvania office of the Erie Area Chamber of Commerce at 814-454-7191.

PRESQUE ISLE NORTH PIER LIGHT

PRESQUE ISLE NORTH PIER LIGHT
Erie, Pennsylvania - Seaway Trail Pennsylvania
1857

Presque Isle North Pier Light has guided commercial and pleasure mariners into Erie Harbor since 1857. After construction, the 30 foot tower was moved twice, the last time in the 1940s when it was relocated to its present location at the east end of the North Pier. During the 1940 reconstruction, the tower was boxed in with heavy steel plating. Early in the last century the light was located on the grounds of the US Life Saving Station just east of the current US Coast Guard station.

Originally fitted with a 4th order Fresnel lens, the light now displays a 2.5 flashing red light emitted by a modern plastic lens. It is maintained by the Coast Guard. The original lens was donated to the Erie County Historical Society in 1995.

Fog signals have been associated with this light from its construction until 1996 when the Coast Guard removed the signal apparatus. Electronic sensors now turn the light on and off depending on the visibility. Besides responding to darkness, the light also comes on during times of heavy fog.

Lightkeeper Charles Waldo served at nearby Presque Isle Lighthouse, built in 1872. In 1876, his wife Mary gave birth to a daughter, Nellie, the first child known to be born at Presque Isle. Early lightkeepers were paid a total of $520 per year for 365 days of service.

Presque Isle North Pier Light can be seen from land and water. The light is near the US Coast Guard Station at Presque Isle State Park. Motorists and bicyclists can take PA Rt. 832 into the Park and watch for a sign to the Coast Guard Station. Travel past the Coast Guard Station to the pier parking area. The light is on the east end of the pier.

For more information, visit The Nature Shop at Presque Isle State Park or call 814-836-9107.

The Nature Shop at Presque Isle and the Presque Isle Partnership supplied the above information. The illustration to the right was reprinted with the permission of artist David L. Tousey.

PRESQUE ISLE LIGHT STATION, ERIE, PA

PRESQUE ISLE LIGHT STATION
Erie, PA - Seaway Trail Pennsylvania
1872

Presque Isle Light Station was needed to warn mariners of the seven-mile long peninsula jutting into Lake Erie on an otherwise straight coastline and to provide them with a location marker as they traveled through the lake. Commissioned in 1870 by the U.S. Lighthouse Service, it replaced Erie Light Station, commonly called the Land Lighthouse.

Construction began in September 1872 with materials first brought to the project by boat. A scow carrying 6,000 bricks was lost, causing builders to find a new method of delivering materials. A crude roadway connecting the station with Misery Bay on the city side of the peninsula allowed safer access. This 1.5 mile road was later planked. A concrete strip laid in 1925 is visible today as Presque Isle State Park's "Sidewalk Trail." When construction halted December 8th, residence and tower masonry was well underway, the residence was roofed, and the tower covered. Construction resumed in April. The $15,000 station was completed July 1, 1873. First keeper Charles Waldo wrote on July 12, 1873: "This is a new station and a light will be exhibited for the first time tonight - there was one visitor."

Constructed of brick, five courses thick, the 57' tower is square outside and round on the inside. The thickness protects against fierce lake storms. The 78 iron steps to the lantern room were forged in Pittsburgh. The original 4th order Fresnel lens was first fueled by whale oil and kerosene. Electrified in the 1920s, a 150-watt bulb ran on batteries charged by diesel generators. Its alternating red and white light caused locals to call this the "Flashlight." In 1962 a modern aircraft-type beacon was installed. Today's light, a 250-watt bulb inside a plastic optic lens, is fully-automated and maintained by the Coast Guard.

Children at the station walked to the bay and were picked up by the Lifesaving Service who rowed them across to Erie. In winter, they walked or skated across the ice to school. Before cars and a road onto the peninsula (1927), the station was often referred to as "the loneliest place on earth."

Presque Isle Light Station was transferred from the federal government to the State of Pennsylvania in June 1998. Presque Isle State Park maintains the residence as employee housing. The Coast Guard maintains the light and tower. A small metal and brick building is the oil shed, once supplied twice a year by the Lighthouse Service. As a precaution against fire, keepers brought only one night's oil supply into the light each night.

Presque Isle Light Station is found at Presque Isle State Park, a National Natural Landmark, by taking PA Route 832 or by boat. A 13-mile road loops around the peninsula and the park's 3,200 acres. The peninsula extends from the mainland four miles west of downtown Erie. For more information, call 814-833-7424.

FOR FURTHER READING

A History of Lighthouses by Patrick Beaver, Citadel Press: Secaucus, New Jersey, 1973.

Along the Trail and Into the Past by Anne E. Hutchinson, St. Lawrence-Eastern Ontario Commission: Watertown, New York, 1986, now distributed by Seaway Trail, Inc.

America's Lighthouses: Their Illustrated History since 1716 by Francis Ross Holland, Jr., Dover: New York, 1988.

Erie Link to the Great Lakes, by Carl B. Lechner, Erie County Historical Society, Erie, Pennsylvania, 1994.

Guide to Great American Lighthouses by Francis Ross Holland, Jr., Preservation Press: Washington, D.C., 1989.

The Lighthouse by Dudley Witney, New York Graphic Society: Boston, 1975.

Lighthouses and Lightships of the United States by George R. Putnam, Houghton-Mifflin Co.: Boston, 1917.

Nautical Seaway Trail Chartbook & Waterfront Guide, Blue Heron Enterprises, Hammond, New York, 1991, now distributed by Seaway Trail, Inc.

The Northern Lights by Charles K. Hyde, Two Peninsula Press: Lansing, Michigan, 1986.

Seaway Trail Bicycling by Bikecentennial, Seaway Trail, Inc.: Sackets Harbor, New York, 1987.

Seaway Trail Guide to the War of 1812 by Patrick Wilder, Seaway Trail, Inc.: Sackets Harbor, New York, 1987.

Seaway Trail Rocks and Landscapes by Ernest H. Muller and Donald Pair, Seaway Trail, Inc.: Sackets Harbor, New York, 1987.

Seaway Trail Wildguide to Natural History by Donald D. Cox, Seaway Trail Foundation, Inc.: Sackets Harbor, New York, 1996.

Keeper's Notes...

Keeper's Notes . . .

*Please use the space below to record your visits
to the publicly-accessible lights along the Seaway Trail.*

Lighthouse	Date Visited	Notes
Dunkirk Historical Light, Dunkirk	5/30/02	Nice exhibits on grounds
Buffalo Main Light, Buffalo		
Old Fort Niagara, Youngstown		
Thirty Mile Point, Barker	6/04	Nice State Park - 6:22 pm closed
Charlotte-Genesee, Rochester	6/04	
Old Sodus, Sodus Point	5/02	Nice museum, climbed to top
Selkirk, Port Ontario		
Tibbetts Point, Cape Vincent		
Erie Land, Erie, PA	5/02	
Presque Isle, Erie, PA	5/02	

Barcelona   5/02   Private Home

Come Explore the Seaway Trail
New York State's Only National Scenic Byway

New York State's Seaway Trail is a scenic driving and boating route which parallels the St. Lawrence River, Lake Ontario, Niagara River and Lake Erie. A world of interesting travel experiences await travelers.

If you're interested in the cultures that helped shape the region's history, you will find museums and attractions detailing the lives of such notable individuals as suffragette Susan B. Anthony, castle builder George Boldt, carousel maker Allen Herschell, Underground Railroad leader Harriet Tubman, artist Frederic Remington, and U.S. Secretary of State William Henry Seward.

Other sites chronicle the contributions of bicycle makers, cobblestone masons, St. Lawrence skiff builders, Shakers, War of 1812 and post-Civil War soldiers, Great Lakes captains, and lighthouse keepers. One of man's greatest engineering feats is seen in the St. Lawrence Seaway where the oceangoing ships of the world have been raised and lowered 42' since 1959.

Active travelers will find the Trail offers access to boating, swimming, bicycling, skiing, snowmobiling, amusement parks, and camping. Lake and river anglers come from around the world for our world-class fishing. Nature lovers find 20% of New York State's Important Bird Areas along the Seaway Trail plus nature centers, zoos, aquaria, and wildlife refuges with trails to walk, bike, ski and canoe.

For a taste of regional cuisine, restaurants across the Trail offer dishes prepared with fresh produce from local farms. Many farmsites and wineries also offer tours and tastings, and have animals for petting, pumpkins for painting, apples for picking, and delicious taste treats year'round.

Year'round events celebrate with flowers, foods, fireworks, pirates, parades, tall ships, tomatoes, court jesters, comediennes, music and all manner of merriment. Niagara Falls' Festival of Lights in November-December and Oswego's Harborfest in July have been voted among America's best events. Jefferson County hosts the nation's oldest continuously-operating county fair. The Erie County Fair is America's second largest fair. The Clothesline Festival in Rochester is one of the largest outdoor art shows in the US.

For travel planning assistance and a free *JOURNEY* magazine, call 1-800-SEAWAY-T, email: info@seawaytrail.com or check www.seawaytrail.com.

Welcome to the Seaway Trail Discovery Center!

The Seaway Trail Discovery Center began welcoming visitors in July 2000. This three-story limestone building was constructed in 1817 as the Union Hotel. A young U.S. Army Lieutenant Ulysses S. Grant often visited here to play checkers. An animated U.S. Grant now greets you as you enter the cultural exhibit which was the hotel's tavern room.

Nine rooms showcase exhibits detailing the Seaway Trail's historic lighthouses, recreational activities, coastal agriculture, and natural resources. In the third floor orientation room, come "ride" along the Seaway Trail as you view a windshield video screen. A camping tent and St. Lawrence skiff beckon you to enjoy the Trail's recreational opportunities.

Beautifully-colored murals depicting Seaway Trail water and landscapes adorn the walls throughout the building. Can you find a blue heron, a cotton-tailed rabbit, or a cattail among the paintings of woodlands, wetlands, sand dunes and fields?

Have you ever imagined yourself as the captain of a tall ship? Have your picture taken at our ship's wheel in the maritime history room, or sit and watch a video detailing the fascinating role of lighthouses along the 500-plus-mile Seaway Trail shoreline. War of 1812 exhibits show artifacts from the Trail's past shaped by soldiers, sailors, and shipbuilders.

If you're a fan of Frank Lloyd Wright, cobblestone masonry or Federal-style buildings, you'll want to linger before the 14 panels of the architecture exhibit. Would you like to know more about the dairy industry? The 8-foot-tall Discovery Center Dairy Cow is waiting in her coastal agriculture room alcove "stall" to tell you all about her life along the Seaway Trail. Exhibits here will whet your appetite for traveling to sites offering the freshest strawberries, sweet corn and apples.

A first-floor gift shop provides a shopping opportunity to find a special souvenir of your visit to the Seaway Trail Discovery Center.

Come sign our guest book soon!

The Seaway Trail Discovery Center is a New York State-owned historic structure operated by the Seaway Trail Foundation.

63

Seaway Trail Publications

Nautical Seaway Trail Chartbook & Waterfront Guide
This "Boater's Atlas" contains 52 NOAA charts for the St. Lawrence River, Lake Ontario, Niagara River, and Lake Erie, lists 600+ waterfront services, and includes emergency and Customs information in an 11" x 17" spiral-bound format. Useful for boaters and RV'ers.

Seaway Trail Bicycling
Interested in traveling the eastern half of the Seaway Trail by bicycle? This 8-piece packet includes an 111-page guidebook to traveling the Trail from Fair Haven to Massena, and maps to six loop tours which lead you to a fish hatchery, historic battlefield, lighthouse, and three nature-filled areas.

Seaway Trail Guide to the War of 1812
Military historian Patrick Wilder has written a concise guide to the fascinating conflict which was the War of 1812. This illustrated guide details 42 significant points located along New York State's Seaway Trail and includes a chronology of events and an important names index.

Seaway Trail Lighthouses 3rd Edition
The book you have in hand details more than two dozen historic lighthouses found along the Seaway Trail in New York State and Pennsylvania. This book makes an excellent gift!

Seaway Trail Wildguide to Natural History
Author Dr. Donald D. Cox and artist Shirley Peron have created a easy-to-read, beautifully-illustrated guide to the diverse plants, birds and wildlife to be seen along the Seaway Trail. More than ten dozen sites including nature centers, wildlife refuges, birdwatching spots, hiking/biking/canoe trails, zoos, aquaria, and parks are listed in this 176-page guide.

For guidebook prices, information on traveling the Seaway Trail, and a free JOURNEY Magazine, call 800-SEAWAY-T or check the web at www.seawaytrail.com.

SEAWAY TRAIL LIGHTHOUSES

*Visit over 20 historic lights along New York State's
454-mile signed scenic highway.*

1. **Barcelona Lighthouse** (1829)
   Private • Barcelona, NY
2. **Historic Dunkirk Lighthouse** (1875)
   Private, Not-for-profit (M/G) • Dunkirk, NY
3. **Buffalo Main Light** (1833)
   Public (P) • Buffalo, NY
4. **Old Fort Niagara Lighthouse** (1872)
   Public (G/P) • Youngstown, NY
5. **Thirty Mile Point Lighthouse** (1875)
   Public (M/C/P)• Barker, NY
6. **Braddock Point Lighthouse** (1896)
   Private • Hilton, NY
7. **Charlotte-Genesee Lighthouse** (1822, 1863)
   Public (M/G/P) • Rochester, NY
8. **Old Sodus Lighthouse** (1870-71)
   Public (M/G/P) • Sodus Point, NY
9. **Oswego West Pierhead Light** (1934)
   Private • Oswego, NY
10. **Selkirk Lighthouse** (1838)
    Private (G/P/A) • Port Ontario, NY
11. **Stony Point Lighthouse** (1869)
    Private • Henderson Harbor, NY
12. **Galoo Island Lighthouse** (1867)
    Private • Henderson Harbor, NY
13. **Charity Shoal Lighthouse** (rebuilt 1929)
    Private • Cape Vincent, NY
14. **Horse Island Lighthouse** (1870)
    Private • Sackets Harbor, NY
15. **Tibbetts Point Lighthouse** (rebuilt 1854)
    Public (A/M/G/P) • Cape Vincent, NY
16. **Rock Island Lighthouse** (1882)
    Public (P) • Fishers Landing, NY
17. **Sunken Rock Lighthouse** (1847)
    Private • Alexandria Bay, NY
18. **Sisters Island Lighthouse** (1870)
    Private • Chippewa Bay, NY
19. **Crossover Island Lighthouse** (1882)
    Private • Chippewa Bay, NY
20. **Ogdensburg Harbor Lighthouse** (1900)
    Private • Ogdensburg, NY

Key: *M=museum; G=gift shop; C=camping; P=picnicking
A=overnight accommodations;*

*Please respect the privacy and property of all non-public
lighthouse owners. Do not trespass on private property.*

*In memory of Shirley Hamblen, Cape Vincent, New York,
who painted this map.*

*This brochure was made possible by a Federal Highway
Administration ISTEA grant administered through the
NYS Department of Transportation to Seaway Trail, Inc.*

Seawa
Light

CANADA

LAKE ONTARI

5.

4.

6.

ROC

3.

NYS T

SEAWAY
TRAIL

2.

For more infor

SEAWA
P. O. Bo
Sackets
1-800-S

LAKE ERIE

1.

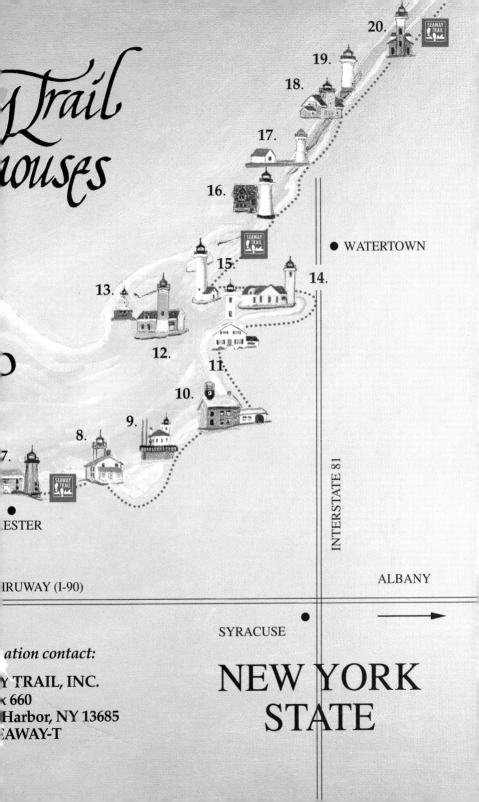